Igor Stravinsky

A COMPLETE CATALOGUE

Compiled by
Clifford Cæsar

1982

San Francisco Press, Inc.

Box 6800, San Francisco, CA 94101-6800, USA

Printed in the U.S.A.

Endpaper portraits by Picasso

ISBN 0-911302-41-7

Library of Congress Catalog Card No. 81-51157

Prefatory Note

This catalogue was compiled in order to bring up to date, and to a certain extent clarify, the information given in the catalogue issued in June 1957 in London (and later, with addenda, in 1962) by Boosey & Hawkes Ltd. With three exceptions (*Three Movements from Petrouchka* for two pianos, *Madrid*, and *Circus Polka*) the present catalogue excludes arrangements and transcriptions unless they were made by the composer himself or in collaboration with him.

Works are listed in chronological order, except where the composer subsequently made transcriptions of excerpts from a larger work; these transcriptions are listed under the main title of the work. Other, more substantial reworkings that were given new titles by the composer are placed chronologically and crossreferenced. The dates given to individual works merely indicate the year of completion. Exact datings of the complete œuvre could not be attempted at this stage without a detailed and coordinated examination of all MS scores, sketches, and marked proofs.

Main titles are given in the language in which they appear on the latest available printed copies: secondary and/or descriptive titles are given in English throughout. Russian titles, where they have not been translated in later editions, are presented in transliteration together with a suggested English translation in parenthesis.

Durations are approximate, but an attempt has been made to compare timings of recordings and live performances with those given in the printed scores, which are in many cases inaccurate.

Details of instrumentation follow the pattern used in Boosey & Hawkes composer catalogues: woodwind doublings and the keys of transposing instruments are indicated only for ensemble or chamber works. The number of players required for percussion instruments has been verified and given in brackets wherever possible. Again, in a number of printed scores the instrumentation list is inaccurate.

Details of first performances have been culled from many sources and crosschecked, where possible, with publishers' records.

Dedications are set out in single quotes and reproduce the printed orthography even where that may conflict with a subsequent listing. A few dedications have never appeared in the printed scores and are to be found in other sources: *An Autobiography (Chroniques de ma vie)* and the Craft-Stravinsky 'Conversations' books.* They are printed in this catalogue without quotation marks.

Piano reductions and vocal scores are by the composer unless otherwise stated. The distinction between a reduction for piano duet (i.e., 1 piano 4 hands) and for 2 pianos (i.e., 2 pianos 4 hands) has been maintained throughout.

The publisher's preference for 'Pocket Score,' 'Miniature Score,' or 'Study Score' has been followed in this catalogue.

Where the copyright of a work has been subsequently assigned to another publishing house, the name of the original publisher is given here in italics.

Two books fundamental to Stravinsky studies have been constant and welcome guides to compilation: *Stravinsky: The Composer and His Works* by Eric Walter White

---

Conversations with Igor Stravinsky (1959); *Memories and Commentaries* (1960); *Expositions and Developments* (1962); *Dialogues and a Diary* (1963); *Themes and Episodes* (1966); *Retrospectives and Conclusions* (1969).

(Faber and Faber, London; University of California Press, Berkeley and Los Angeles, 1966 and 1979) and *Stravinsky in Pictures and Documents* by Vera Stravinsky and Robert Craft (Simon and Schuster, New York, 1978; Hutchinson, London, 1979).

I would like to express my gratitude to the staff of Boosey & Hawkes Ltd., J. & W. Chester Ltd., and Schott & Co. Ltd. for their unstinting help and patient guidance during the compilation of this catalogue.

Clifford Cæsar

London, 1981

Igor Stravinsky's Publishers

ASSOCIATED MUSIC PUBLISHERS INC.
New York

M. P. BELAIEV
Paris - Bonn

W. BESSEL
St. Petersburg

BOOSEY & HAWKES
London - New York - Paris - Bonn - Toronto - Sydney - Johannesburg - Mölndal

BREITKOPF & HÄRTEL
Leipzig

J. & W. CHESTER
London

FABER MUSIC LTD.
London

ROBERT FORBERG
Bad Godesberg

WILHELM HANSEN
Copenhagen

LEEDS MUSIC CORPORATION (MCA MUSIC)
New York

EDWARD B. MARKS MUSIC CO.
New York

MERCURY MUSIC CO.
New York

EDWIN H. MORRIS & CO.
London

B. SCHOTTS SÖHNE
Mainz - London

Contents

Stravinsky's autograph of his *Hommage à Nadia Boulanger,* written for her 60th birthday in 1947, published here for the first time. (Copyright © 1982 by Boosey & Hawkes Music Publishers Limited.)

Chronological List of Works

Tarantella
FOR PIANO
1898
Unpublished

Storm Cloud
ROMANCE FOR VOICE AND PIANO
1902
Duration: 1 min
Russian text by Alexander Pushkin
Faber Music

Scherzo
FOR PIANO
1902
Duration: 4 min
'Dedicated to Nicholas Richter'
Faber Music

Sonata in F sharp minor
FOR PIANO
St. Petersburg, 1904
Duration: 32 min
1. Allegro 2. Vivo 3. Andante 4. Allegro
Privately performed by Nicholas Richter to the Rimsky-Korsakov circle on 22 February 1905.

A public performance was later given by Nicholas Richter at one of the Evenings of Contemporary Music, St. Petersburg.
'Dedicated to Nicholas Richter'
Faber Music

Cantata

FOR MIXED CHOIR AND PIANO
1904
Performed by members of the Rimsky-Korsakov circle on 19 March 1904.
Composed for the 60th birthday of N. A. Rimsky-Korsakov.
Unpublished
MS presumed lost

The Mushrooms Going to War

SONG FOR BASS AND PIANO
1904
Boosey & Hawkes

Conductor and Tarantula

SONG FOR VOICE AND PIANO
1906
Performed by members of the Rimsky-Korsakov circle in March 1906.
Unpublished
MS presumed lost

Symphony in E flat, Opus 1

FOR ORCHESTRA
Ustilug, 1907
(rev. 1913)
Duration: 30 min
3.2.3.2. — 4.3.3.1. — Timp. Perc. — Str.
1. Allegro moderato. 2. Scherzo. Allegretto 3. Largo 4. Finale. Allegro molto
First private performance: 27 April 1907. St. Petersburg Court Orchestra. Conductor: H. Wahrlich.
First public performance: 22 January 1908. Belaiev's season of Russian Symphony Concerts, St. Petersburg. Conductor: Felix Blumenfeld.
'Meinem teuren Lehrer Nikolai Andreewitsch Rimsky-Korsakow'
Jurgenson
Rob. Forberg

Faun and Shepherdess, Opus 2

SONG SUITE FOR MEZZO–SOPRANO AND ORCHESTRA

St. Petersburg, 1907

Duration: 10 min

Russian text by Alexander Pushkin
French translation by Alexander Komarov
German translation by Heinrich Möller

3.2.2.2. — 4.2.3.1. — Timp. Perc. — Str.

1. Shepherdess 2. Faun. 3. Torrent

First private performance: 27 April 1907. St. Petersburg Court Orchestra. Conductor: H. Wahrlich.
First public performance: 16 February 1908. Belaiev's season of Russian Symphony Concerts, St. Petersburg. Conductor: Felix Blumenfeld.

Dedicated to Ekaterina Gabrielovna Stravinsky

Reduction for voice and piano
M. P. Belaiev

Pastorale

SONG WITHOUT WORDS FOR SOPRANO AND PIANO

Ustilug, 1907

Duration: 4 min

Performed by members of the Rimsky-Korsakov circle on 31 October 1907.
First public performance: Winter, 1907–08. Evenings of Contemporary Music, St. Petersburg. Elizabeth Petrenko and the composer.

Dedicated to Nadiezhda Rimsky-Korsakov.

Jurgenson
Schott

Transcriptions

  (i) FOR SOPRANO, OBOE, COR ANGLAIS, CLARINET IN A, AND BASSOON
      Biarritz, 1923
      Schott

  (ii) FOR VIOLIN, OBOE, COR ANGLAIS, CLARINET IN A, AND BASSOON
      1933
      Schott

  (iii) FOR VIOLIN AND PIANO
      Transcribed in collaboration with Samuel Dushkin
      1933
      Schott

11

Two Melodies, Opus 6

FOR MEZZO–SOPRANO AND PIANO

Ustilug, 1907–08

Duration: 8 min

Russian text by Serge Gorodetzky
German translation by Serge Gorodetzky
French translation by M. D. Calvocoressi
English translation by M. D. Calvocoressi

1. Spring (The Cloister)
   Dedicated to Elizabeth Petrenko
2. A Song of the Dew (Mystic Song of the Ancient Russian Flagellants)
   Dedicated to Serge Gorodetzky

First performance: Winter, 1907–08. Evenings of Contemporary Music, St. Petersburg. Elizabeth Petrenko and the composer.

Jurgenson
Boosey & Hawkes

Scherzo Fantastique, Opus 3

FOR ORCHESTRA

Ustilug, 1908
(rev. 1930)

Duration: 12 min

4.3.4.3. — 4.3.0.0. — Cymbals, Celesta, 3 (rev. 2) Harps — Str.

First performance: 6 February 1909. Siloti Concerts, St. Petersburg. Conductor: Alexander Siloti.

Dedicated to Alexander Siloti

Study score. Full score and parts for hire.

Jurgenson
Schott

Fireworks, Opus 4

A FANTASY FOR ORCHESTRA

Ustilug, 1908

Duration: 4 min

3.2.3.2. — 6.3.3.1. — Timp. Perc. (4), Celesta, 2 Harps — Str. (16.14.12.10.8.)

First performance: 6 February 1909. Siloti Concerts, St. Petersburg. Conductor: Alexander Siloti.

'Nadia und Maximilian Steinberg gewidmet'

Study score. Full score and parts for hire.

Schott

Chant funèbre, Opus 5

FOR WIND INSTRUMENTS

Ustilug, 1908

First performance: 13 February 1909. Grand Hall of the St. Petersburg Conservatory. Conductor: Felix Blumenfeld.

In memory of N. A. Rimsky-Korsakov

Unpublished

MS presumed lost

Four Studies, Opus 7

FOR PIANO

Ustilug, 1908

Duration: 8 min

1. Con moto
   'À E. Mitusov'
2. Allegro brillante
   'À Nicholas Richter'
3. Andantino
   'À André Rimsky-Korsakov'
4. Vivo
   'À Vladimir Rimsky-Korsakov'

Jurgenson
Anton J. Benjamin
Boosey & Hawkes

Kobold (Edvard Grieg)

ORCHESTRATED BY STRAVINSKY

At Diaghilev's request, for the score of *Le Festin*

First performance: January 1909. Maryinsky Theater, St. Petersburg.

Produced by the Russian Ballet on 19 May 1909 at the Théâtre du Châtelet, Paris.

Unpublished

Nocturne in A flat and Valse brillante in E flat (Frédéric Chopin)

ORCHESTRATED BY STRAVINSKY

At Diaghilev's request, for the score of *Les Sylphides*

Produced by the Russian Ballet on 2 June 1909 at the Théâtre du Châtelet, Paris.

Unpublished

Mephistopheles' Lied vom Floh (Ludwig van Beethoven, Opus 75, no. 3)

TRANSCRIBED FOR BASS AND ORCHESTRA BY STRAVINSKY

1909

Duration: 3 min

German text from Goethe's *Faust*

2.2.2.2. — 2.0.0.0. — Str.

Full score and parts for hire

Boosey & Hawkes

Chanson de Méphistophélès dans la cave d'Auerbach (Modeste Mussorgsky)

TRANSCRIBED FOR BARITONE OR BASS AND ORCHESTRA BY STRAVINSKY

1910

Duration: 3 min

Setting of a French translation of Goethe's text by M. D. Calvocoressi
German translation by A. Bernhard
English translation by Rosa Newmarch

3.2.2.2. — 4.2.3.1. — Timp. — Str.

This orchestration and the preceding one were both made for a 'Goethe-in-music' concert in St. Petersburg, conducted by Alexander Siloti.

Full score and parts for hire

W. Bessel
Boosey & Hawkes

L'Oiseau de feu — The Firebird

BALLET IN TWO SCENES AFTER THE RUSSIAN FAIRY STORY

Scenario by Michel Fokine

St. Petersburg, 1910

Duration: 45 min

4.4.4.4. — 4.3.3.1. — Timp. Perc. (4), Celesta, 3 Harps, Piano — Str. (16.16.14.8.8.)

Stage band: 3 trumpets, 2 tenor tubas, 2 bass tubas, 2 bells

First performance: 25 June 1910. Russian Ballet, Théâtre de l'Opéra, Paris. Conductor: Gabriel Pierné. Choreography: Michel Fokine. Décor: Alexander Golovine. Costumes: Alexander Golovine and Léon Bakst.

'À André Rimsky-Korsakov'

Piano reduction. Full score.

Full score and parts for hire.

Jurgenson
Schott

(L'Oiseau de feu, Cont'd)

Concert Suites

(i) Concert Suite

FOR ORCHESTRA

1911

Duration: 21 min

4.4.4.4. — 4.3.3.1. — Timp. Perc. (4), Celesta, 3 Harps, Piano — Str.

Jurgenson

(ii) Concert Suite

FOR ORCHESTRA

1919

Duration: 22 min

2.2.2.2. — 4.2.3.1. — Timp. Perc. (5), Harp, Piano — Str.

Full score. Study score.

Full score and parts for hire.

Schott (for Germany)

J. & W. Chester (for UK)

(iii) Ballet Suite

FOR ORCHESTRA

1945

Duration: 28 min

2.2.2.2. — 4.2.3.1. — Timp. Perc. (3), Harp, Piano — Str.

Study score.

Full score and parts for hire.

Schott (for Germany)

Leeds Music Corporation (for USA)

J. & W. Chester (for UK)

Transcriptions

(i) Prélude et ronde des princesses

FOR VIOLIN AND PIANO

1929

'Dédié à Paul Kochanski'

Schott

(ii) Berceuse

FOR VIOLIN AND PIANO

1929

'Dédié à Paul Kochanski'

Schott

(iii) Berceuse

FOR VIOLIN AND PIANO

In collaboration with Samuel Dushkin

1933

Schott

(L'Oiseau de feu, Cont'd)

(iv) Scherzo
FOR VIOLIN AND PIANO
In collaboration with Samuel Dushkin
1933
Schott

Two Songs, Opus 9
FOR BARITONE AND PIANO
La Baule, 1910
Duration: 4 min
French texts by Paul Verlaine
Russian translation by Stepan Mitusov
English translation by M. D. Calvocoressi
German translation by M. D. Calvocoressi
1. Sagesse ('Un grand sommeil noir . . .')
2. La Bonne chanson ('La lune blanche . . .')
'À mon frère Goury'
Jurgenson
Boosey & Hawkes

Transcription
FOR BARITONE AND SMALL ORCHESTRA
Partially orchestrated at La Baule, Summer 1910
Newly orchestrated, and completed, in 1951
2.0.2.0. — 2.0.0.0. — Str.
Vocal score. Full score.
Full score and parts for hire.
Boosey & Hawkes

Petrouchka — Петрушка
BURLESQUE IN FOUR SCENES
Scenario by Igor Stravinsky and Alexandre Benois
Rome, 1911
(rev. Hollywood, 1945–47; reprinted with corrections 1965)
Duration: 38 min

16

(Petrouchka, Cont'd)

Original version of 1911:
4.4.4.4. — 4.4.3.1. — Timp. Perc. (6), Celesta, 2 Harps, Piano — Str.

Revised version of 1947:
3.3.3.3. — 4.4.3.1. — Timp. Perc. (4), Celesta, Harp, Piano — Str.

First performance: 13 June 1911. Russian Ballet, Théâtre du Châtelet, Paris. Conductor: Pierre Monteux. Choreography: Michel Fokine. Décor and costumes: Alexandre Benois

'À Alexandre Benois'

Original version:
Full score and parts for hire (except USA).

Revised version:
Reduction for piano duet. Full score. Pocket score.
Full score and parts for hire.

Edition Russe de Musique
Boosey & Hawkes

Transcriptions

  (i) Three Movements from Petrouchka

FOR PIANO

1921

1. Russian Dance   2. Petrouchka's cell   3. The Shrove-tide Fair

First performance (under the subtitle 'Sonata'): 26 December 1922. Paris. Jean Wiéner.

'À Arthur Rubinstein'

Edition Russe de Musique
Boosey & Hawkes

 (ii) Russian Dance

FOR VIOLIN AND PIANO

In collaboration with Samuel Dushkin

1932

Edition Russe de Musique
Boosey & Hawkes

(iii) Three Movements from Petrouchka

FOR TWO PIANOS

Transcribed by Victor Babin

1924

1. Russian Dance   2. Petrouchka's cell   3. The Shrove-tide Fair

The Cadenza was later rewritten by the composer

The three movements are published separately

Boosey & Hawkes

17

Two Poems of Balmont

FOR HIGH VOICE AND PIANO

Ustilug, 1911
(rev. 1947)

Duration: 2½ min

Russian texts by Konstantin Balmont
English translation by Robert Burness
French translation by M. D. Calvocoressi
German translation by Berthold Feiwel

1. The Flower
  'To my mother'
2. The Dove
  'To my sister-in-law Ludmila Beliankin'

Transcription

FOR HIGH VOICE AND CHAMBER ORCHESTRA

1954

2 flutes (2nd doubling piccolo), 2 clarinets in B flat (2nd doubling bass clarinet in B flat), piano, and string quartet

This version includes a new English translation by Robert Craft

Later published together with *Three Japanese Lyrics* (1913)

Full score.
Full score and parts for hire.

Edition Russe de Musique
Boosey & Hawkes

Zvezdoliki — Звѣздоликій — Le Roi des étoiles —The Star-faced One

CANTATA FOR MALE VOICE CHORUS AND ORCHESTRA

Ustilug, 1911–12

Duration: 6 min

Russian text by Konstantin Balmont
French translation by M. D. Calvocoressi
Later scores include a German verse translation by Walther Neft

4.4.4.4. — 8.3.3.1. — Timp. Bass drum, Tam-tam, Celesta, 2 Harps — Str.

First performance: 19 April 1939. Institut Nationale de Radio-diffusion Belge, Brussels. Conductor: Franz André.

'À Claude Debussy'

Vocal score. Full score.

Jurgenson
Rob. Forberg

Three Japanese Lyrics

FOR HIGH VOICE AND PIANO OR CHAMBER ORCHESTRA

Clarens, 1913

Duration: 4 min

2 flutes (2nd doubling piccolo), 2 clarinets in B flat (2nd doubling bass clarinet in B flat), piano, and string quartet

Russian texts, translated from the Japanese, by A. Brandta
French translation by Maurice Delage
English translation by Robert Burness
German translation by Ernst Roth

1. Akahito
   'To Maurice Delage'
2. Mazatsumi
   'To Florent Schmitt'
3. Tsaraiuki
   'To Maurice Ravel'

First performance*: 14 January 1914. Société Musicale Indépendante, Salle Erard, Paris.

Later published together with *Two Poems of Balmont* (1911)

Voice and piano version available separately.
Full score.
Full score and parts for hire.

Edition Russe de Musique
Boosey & Hawkes

Le Sacre du printemps — The Rite of Spring

PICTURES FROM PAGAN RUSSIA IN TWO PARTS

Scenario by Igor Stravinsky and Nicholas Roerich

Clarens, 1913
(rev. 1947; newly engraved and corrected edition 1967)

Duration: 33 min

5.5.5.5. — 8.5.3.2. — Timp. (2), Perc. (3) — Str.

First performance: 29 May 1913. Russian Ballet, Théâtre des Champs-Elysées, Paris.
Conductor: Pierre Monteux. Choreography: Vaslav Nijinsky.

Dedicated to Nicholas Roerich

Reduction for piano duet. Full score. Pocket score.
Full score and parts for hire.

Edition Russe de Musique
Boosey & Hawkes

New instrumentation of 'Danse Sacrale'
1943
Associated Music Publishers, Inc.

---

*Presumably in the chamber orchestra version. The program also included the première of Ravel's *Trois poèmes de Stéphane Mallarmé*.

(Le Sacre du printemps, Cont'd)

Facsimile

Sketches for The Rite of Spring 1911–1913

Interspersed are sketches for *Le Rossignol, Pribaoutki, Three Japanese Lyrics,* and *Souvenir de mon enfance.*
Foreword by François Lesure.
Preface, commentary, and notes on performance by Robert Craft.
Appendix containing letters from Stravinsky to Nicholas Roerich and N. F. Findeizen, and Stravinsky's choreographic notes for Vaslav Nijinsky.
Boosey & Hawkes

Khovanshchina — Хованщина (Modeste Mussorgsky)

ORCHESTRATION BY STRAVINSKY

Orchestrations, in collaboration with Maurice Ravel, of sections of the opera, including the Finale, left incomplete at Mussorgsky's death.
Clarens, 1913

First performance: 5 June 1913. Russian Ballet, Théâtre des Champs-Elysées, Paris.
W. Bessel, St. Petersburg
Breitkopf & Härtel, Leipzig

Trois petites chansons (Souvenir de mon enfance)

FOR VOICE AND PIANO

Begun c. 1906
Definitive version: Clarens, 1913

Duration: 2 min

Russian popular texts
French translation by C. F. Ramuz

1. The Magpie
   'To my son Sviatoslav Soulima'
2. The Rook
   'To my daughter Ludmila'
3. The Jackdaw
   'To my son Theodore'

Edition Russe de Musique
Boosey & Hawkes

Transcription

FOR VOICE AND SMALL ORCHESTRA

Nice, 1929–30

Duration: 3 min

2.2.2.2. — 0.0.0.0. — Strings without double basses

Texts as in the voice and piano version, with an English translation by Robert Burness. All three songs are lengthened.

Full score and parts for hire
Edition Russe de Musique
Boosey & Hawkes

Le Rossignol

LYRIC TALE IN THREE ACTS AFTER HANS CHRISTIAN ANDERSEN

Leysin, 1914
(rev. 1962)
Act 1, Ustilug, 1908–09
Acts 2 and 3, Clarens-Leysin, 1913–14

Duration: 45 min

Russian libretto by Stepan Mitusov
French translation by M. D. Calvocoressi
English translation by Robert Craft
German translation by A. Elukhen and B. Feiwel

3.3.3.3. — 4.4.3.1. — Timp. Perc. (5), Celesta, 2 Harps, Mandolin, Guitar, Piano — Str.

First performance: 26 May 1914. Russian Ballet, Théâtre de l'Opéra, Paris. Conductor: Pierre Monteux. Designer: Alexandre Benois. Choreography: Boris Romanov. Stage production: Alexander Sanin.

Dedicated to Stepan Mitusov

Vocal score. Pocket score. Libretti, English and German.
Full score, vocal score, choral score, and parts for hire.

Edition Russe de Musique
Boosey & Hawkes

VOCAL EXCERPTS

Introduction
Song of the Fisherman — Tenor
Song of the Nightingale — Soprano

Duration: 8 min

3.3.3.3. — 4.3.0.0. — Timp. Perc. Celesta, 2 Harps — Str.

Full score and parts for hire.

Edition Russe de Musique
Boosey & Hawkes

Chant du Rossignol. See below (1917).

Three Pieces for String Quartet

Leysin-Salvan, 1914
(rev. 1918)

Duration: 8 min

First performance: 19 May 1915. Paris.

The 1914 version was dedicated to Charles-Albert Cingria; the 1918 revised score bears the inscription:
'À Ernest Ansermet'

Pocket score. Parts.

Edition Russe de Musique
Boosey & Hawkes

21

(Three Pieces for String Quartet, Cont'd)

Transcriptions

(i) FOR PIANO DUET

1914

Dedicated to Charles-Albert Cingria

Unpublished

(ii) FOR ORCHESTRA

Under the titles *Danse, Excentrique,* and *Cantique,* the Three Pieces form the first three movements of *Quatre Études* for orchestra. See below (1929).

Pribaoutki — Прибаутки— Chansons plaisantes

FOR MEDIUM VOICE AND EIGHT INSTRUMENTS

Salvan-Clarens, 1914

Duration: 5 min

Russian popular texts
French translation by C. F. Ramuz
German translation by R. St. Hoffmann

Flute, oboe (doubling cor anglais), clarinet in A (doubling in B flat), bassoon, violin, viola, violoncello, and double bass.

1. Kornilo — Cornelius
2. Natashka
3. The Colonel
4. The Old Man and the Hare

First performance: 6 June 1919. Society for Private Musical Performances, Vienna.

'À ma femme'

Reduction for voice and piano. Study score.
Full score and parts for hire.

Ad. Henn
J. & W. Chester

Valse des fleurs

FOR TWO PIANOS

Clarens, 1914

Boosey & Hawkes

Three Easy Pieces

FOR PIANO DUET (LEFT HAND EASY)

Clarens—Chateau d'Oex, 1914–15

Duration: 3 min

1. March
   'À Alfredo Casella'
2. Waltz
   'À Erik Satie'
3. Polka
   'À Serge Diaghilev'

(Three Easy Pieces, Cont'd)

First performance: 22 April 1918. Conservatoire de Lausanne. Nino Rossi and Ernest Ansermet.

Ad. Henn
J. & W. Chester

Transcriptions

(i) Polka

Transcribed for cimbalom solo (for the repertory of Aladar Racz) in 1915. Unpublished, but the MS is reproduced to illustrate an article by Mme. Yvonne Racz-Barblon in *Feuilles musicales,* Lausanne, March–April 1962.

(ii) MS version of the March for twelve instruments, dated 25 March 1915. Unpublished.

(iii) March, Waltz and Polka were later orchestrated to form part of the *Suite no. 2* for chamber orchestra. See below (1921).

Souvenir d'une marche Boche
FOR PIANO
Morges, 1915
First printed in facsimile in *The Book of the Homeless (Le Livre des sans-foyer),* edited by Edith Wharton, Macmillan and Co. Ltd., London. 1916.
Boosey & Hawkes

Berceuses du chat
FOR MEDIUM VOICE AND THREE CLARINETS
Clarinets:
1. Clarinet in E flat
2. Clarinet in A doubling clarinet in B flat
3. Clarinet in A doubling bass clarinet in B flat
Clarens-Morges, 1915–16
Duration: 5 min
Russian popular texts
French translation by C. F. Ramuz
German translation by R. St. Hoffmann
1. (Spi kot' — Sleep, cat)
2. (Kot' na pyechi — Cat in the corner)
3. (Bai-bai)
4. (U kota, kota — What a cat has)
First performance: 6 June 1919. Society for Private Performances, Vienna.
Dedicated to Natalie Goncharova and Michel Larionov
Reduction for voice and piano. Study score.
Parts for hire
Ad. Henn
J. & W. Chester

Renard

A BURLESQUE FOR THE STAGE
FOR TWO TENORS, TWO BASSES, AND AN INSTRUMENTAL ENSEMBLE
Morges, 1916
Duration: 20 min
Russian text by the composer based on Russian folk tales
French translation by C. F. Ramuz
German translation by Rupert Koller
English translation by Rollo H. Myers
1.1.1.1. — 2.1.0.0. — Timp. Perc. (2), Cimbalom or Piano — Solo Strings (1.1.1.1.1.)
First performance: 18 May 1922. Russian Ballet, Théâtre de l'Opéra, Paris. Conductor: Ernest Ansermet. Choreography: Bronislava Nijinska. Décor and costumes: Michel Larionov.
'Très respectueusement dédié à Madame la Princesse Edmonde de Polignac'
Vocal score. Study score.
Full score and parts for hire.
Ad. Henn
J. & W. Chester

Five Easy Pieces

FOR PIANO DUET (RIGHT HAND EASY)
Morges, 1917
Duration: 9 min
1. Andante   2. Española   3. Balalaika   4. Napolitana   5. Galop
First performance: 22 April 1918. Conservatoire de Lausanne. Nino Rossi and Ernest Ansermet.
Dedicated to Eugenia Errazuriz
Ad. Henn
J. & W. Chester

Transcription
Four of the Five Pieces were later orchestrated to form the *Suite no. 1* for chamber orchestra. See below (1925).

Chant du rossignol

SYMPHONIC POEM FOR ORCHESTRA
Morges, 1917
Duration: 20 min
2.2.2.2. — 4.3.3.1. — Timp. Perc. (4), 2 Harps, Piano — Str.
Based on Acts 2 and 3 of *Le Rossignol*. The piano reduction is prefaced by a synopsis of Andersen's Tale, headed as follows:
1. The Fête in the Emperor of China's Palace
2. The Two Nightingales
3. Illness and Recovery of the Emperor of China

(Chant du rossignol, Cont'd)

First performance: 6 December 1919. Orchestre de la Suisse Romande, Geneva. Conducted by Ernest Ansermet

Piano reduction. Pocket score.

Full score and parts for hire.

Edition Russe de Musique

Boosey & Hawkes

Transcription

Songs of the Nightingale and Chinese March

FOR VIOLIN AND PIANO

In collaboration with Samuel Dushkin

Voreppe, 1932

Edition Russe de Musique

Boosey & Hawkes

Le Rossignol. See above (1913).

Trois histoires pour enfants

FOR VOICE AND PIANO

Morges, 1915–17

Duration: 5 min

Russian popular texts

French translation by C. F. Ramuz

English translation of 1 by Rosa Newmarch

1. Tilim-bom
2. Geese and Swans
3. (Medved' — The Bear)

'Pour mon fils cadet'

J. & W. Chester

Transcriptions

Tilim-bom

FOR VOICE AND ORCHESTRA

Biarritz, 1923

Duration: 1 min

3.2.2.0. — 2.1.0.0. — Timp. — Str.

This is a lengthened version with additional words by the composer.

First performance: 7 January 1924. Antwerp. Conducted by the composer.

Full score and parts for hire.

J. & W. Chester

Songs 1 and 2 were transcribed in 1954, and form part of Four Songs for voice, flute, harp, and guitar. See below (1954).

Valse pour les enfants
FOR PIANO
Morges, 1916–17
Duration: 1 min
First published, in facsimile, in *Le Figaro (Supplement littéraire)*, 21 May 1922.

Boosey & Hawkes

Chant des bateliers du Volga
FOR WIND INSTRUMENTS AND PERCUSSION
Arranged by Stravinsky at Diaghilev's request
Rome, 1917
Duration: 2 min
2.2.2.3. — 4.3.3.1. — Timp. Bass drum, Tam-tam
First performance: April 1917. Costanzi Theater, Rome.
Full score and parts for hire.
J. & W. Chester

Podblyudnya — Подблюдныя — Four Russian Peasant Songs ('Saucers')
FOR FEMALE VOICES A CAPPELLA
Salvan-Morges, 1914–17
Duration: 4 min
Words after Afanasiev's collection of Russian popular texts
A phonetic Russian text prepared by the composer
French translation (anonymous)
English translation (anonymous)
German translation by Hermann Roth
1. On Saints' Days in Chigisakh
2. Ovsen
3. The Pike
4. Master Portly
First performance: 1917. Geneva. Conductor: Vassily Kibalchich.
Schott (for Germany)
J. & W. Chester (for UK)
Edward B. Marks Music Corp. (for USA)

New version
FOR FEMALE VOICES ACCOMPANIED BY FOUR HORNS
1954
First performance: 11 October 1954. Monday Evening Concerts, Los Angeles.
Conductor: Robert Craft.
Chorus part, with reduction.
Instrumental parts for hire.
Schott (for Germany)
J. & W. Chester (for UK)

Canons for Two Horns
1917
Unpublished
MS presented to Dr. Roux, Geneva. Presumed lost.

Étude
FOR PIANOLA
Les Diablerets-Morges, 1917
Duration: 2 min 15 sec
First audition: 13 October 1921. Aeolian Hall, London.
Dedicated to Madame Eugenia Errazuriz
Published, as a Pianola roll, by the Aeolian Company Ltd., London.
The MS is set out on six staves per system
Boosey & Hawkes

Transcriptions
  (i) Madrid
       FOR TWO PIANOS
       Transcribed by Soulima Stravinsky
       Boosey & Hawkes
 (ii) Étude, orchestrated under the title *Madrid,* forms the fourth of *Quatre Études* for
       orchestra. See below (1929).

Berceuse
FOR VOICE AND PIANO
Morges, 1917
Duration: 45 sec
Russian text by the composer
French translation by C. F. Ramuz
'À ma fillette'
Published as Appendix A to *Expositions and Developments,* Faber and Faber, London,
1962.

Histoire du soldat
TO BE READ, PLAYED, AND DANCED
Three speaking roles, dancer, and seven instrumentalists
Morges, 1918
Duration: 50–60 min
French libretto by C. F. Ramuz
Two English translations:
 (i) by Rosa Newmarch
(ii) by Michael Flanders and Kitty Black
German translation by Hans Reinhart
Clarinet in A doubling in B flat, bassoon, cornet in A doubling in B flat, trombone, percussion (one player), violin, double bass.
First performance: 28 September 1918. Théâtre Municipal de Lausanne. Conductor: Ernest Ansermet. Décor and costumes: René Auberjonois.
'À Werner Reinhart'

Piano reduction. Full score. Study score. Libretti, French, English, and German. Full score and parts for hire.
J. & W. Chester

Concert Suite
1920
Duration: 35 min
Clarinet in A doubling in B flat, bassoon, cornet in A doubling in B flat, trombone, percussion (one player), violin, double bass.
1. The Soldier's March   2. The Soldier's Violin   3. Royal March   4. The Little Concert
5. Tango — Waltz — Ragtime   6. The Devil's Dance   7. Chorale   8. The Devil's Triumphal March
First performance: 20 July 1920. Wigmore Hall, London. Conductor: Ernest Ansermet.
Full score and parts for hire.
J. & W. Chester

Transcription
Suite from L'Histoire du soldat
FOR CLARINET IN A DOUBLING IN B FLAT, VIOLIN, AND PIANO
1918–19
Duration: 25 min
1. The Soldier's March   2. The Soldier's Violin   3. The Little Concert   4. Tango — Waltz — Ragtime   5. The Devil's Dance
First performance: 8 November 1919. Conservatoire de Lausanne. Edmond Allegra, José Porta, and José Iturbi.
'Dédiée à Monsieur Werner Reinhart'
J. & W. Chester

Ragtime
FOR ELEVEN INSTRUMENTS
Morges, 1918
Duration: 4½ min
Flute, clarinet in A, horn, cornet in B flat, trombone, percussion (one player), cimbalom, two violins, viola, double bass.
First performance: 27 April 1920. The Philharmonic Quartet and a small orchestra, Aeolian Hall, London. Conductor: Arthur Bliss.
'À Madame E. Errazuriz'
Piano reduction. Study score.
Full score and parts for hire.
J. & W. Chester

Three Pieces
FOR CLARINET SOLO
Morges, 1918
Duration: 4 min
Nos. 1 and 2 for clarinet in A
No. 3 for clarinet in B flat
1. ♩ = 52   2. ♪ = 168   3. ♪ = 160
First performance: 8 November 1919. Conservatoire de Lausanne. Edmond Allegra.
Dedicated to Werner Reinhart
J. & W. Chester

Prologue from Boris Godunov (Modeste Mussorgsky)
TRANSCRIBED FOR PIANO BY STRAVINSKY
(The Chorus of the Prologue only)
Morges, 1918
Boosey & Hawkes

Lied ohne Namen
FOR TWO BASSOONS
1918
Duration: 1 min
First performance: 30 October 1979. Queen Elizabeth Hall, London. John Price and Joanna Graham.
Boosey & Hawkes

La Marseillaise (Claude Joseph Rouget de Lisle)
TRANSCRIBED FOR UNACCOMPANIED VIOLIN BY STRAVINSKY
Morges, 1919
Duration: 1 min 40 sec
First performance: 13 November 1979. Queen Elizabeth Hall, London. Kyung-Wha Chung.
Boosey & Hawkes

Four Russian Songs
FOR VOICE AND PIANO
Morges, 1918–19
Duration: 5 min
Russian popular texts
French translation by C. F. Ramuz
1. The Drake
2. (Zapevnaya — [Introductory] Song)
3. (Podblyudnaya — Saucer-riddle)
4. A Russian Spiritual
First performance: 7 February 1920. Salle Gaveau, Paris. Mme. Koubitzky as soloist.
Dedicated to Maja and Bela Strozzi-Pečić
J. & W. Chester

Transcription
Nos. 1 and 4 form part of *Four Songs* for voice, flute, harp, and guitar. See below (1954).

Piano-Rag-Music
FOR PIANO
Morges, 1919
Duration: 3 min
First performance: 8 November 1919. Conservatoire de Lausanne. José Iturbi.
'Dédié à Arthur Rubinstein'
J. & W. Chester

Pulcinella
BALLET IN ONE ACT, BASED ON THEMES AND FRAGMENTS BY GIAMBATTISTA PERGOLESI
FOR SMALL ORCHESTRA, WITH SOPRANO, TENOR, AND BASS SOLI
Morges, 1920
(rev. 1965)
Duration: 35 min
Italian texts
2.2.0.2. — 2.1.1.0. — concertino strings (1.1.1.1.1.)
 ripieno strings (4.4.4.3.3.)
First performance: 15 May 1920. Russian Ballet, Théâtre de l'Opéra, Paris. Conductor: Ernest Ansermet. Choreography: Léonide Massine. Décor and costumes: Pablo Picasso.
Vocal score published by J. & W. Chester
Full score and parts for hire from:
Edition Russe de Musique
Boosey & Hawkes

Pulcinella
SUITE FOR ORCHESTRA
c. 1922
(rev. 1949)
Duration: 22 min
2.2.0.2. — 2.1.1.0. concertino strings (1.1.1.1.1.)
                         ripieno strings   (4.4.4.3.3.)
1. Sinfonia (Overture) 2. Serenata 3. Scherzino — Allegro — Andantino
4. Tarantella 5. Toccata 6. Gavotta con due variazioni 7. Vivo 8. Minuetto e finale
First performance: 22 December 1922. Boston Symphony Orchestra. Conducted by Pierre
Monteux.
Pocket score.
Full score and parts for hire.
Edition Russe de Musique
Boosey & Hawkes

Transcriptions
 (i) Suite
      FOR VIOLIN AND PIANO
      1925
      1. Introduzione 2. Serenata 3. Tarantella 4. Gavotta con due variazioni
      5. Minuetto e finale
      Dedicated to Paul Kochanski
 (ii) Suite Italienne
      FOR VIOLONCELLO AND PIANO
      In collaboration with Gregor Piatigorsky
      1932
      1. Introduzione 2. Serenata 3. Aria 4. Tarantella 5. Minuetto e finale
(iii) Suite Italienne
      FOR VIOLIN AND PIANO
      In collaboration with Samuel Dushkin
      c. 1933
      1. Introduzione 2. Serenata 3. Tarantella 4. Gavotta con due variazioni
      5. Minuetto e finale
Edition Russe de Musique
Boosey & Hawkes

Concertino
FOR STRING QUARTET
Carantec-Garches, 1920
Duration: 6 min
First performance: 3 November 1920. New York. Flonzaley Quartet.
'Dédié au Quatuor Flonzaley'

31

(Concertino, Cont'd)
Reduction for piano duet
Study score. Parts.
Wilhelm Hansen

Transcription
Concertino
FOR TWELVE INSTRUMENTS
Transcribed 1952
Duration: 6 min
Flute, oboe, cor anglais, clarinet in A, two bassoons, two trumpets in B flat, trombone, bass trombone, violin obbligato, violoncello obbligato.
First performance: 11 November 1952. Los Angeles Chamber Symphony Orchestra. Conducted by the composer.
Study score.
Full score and parts for hire.
Wilhelm Hansen

Symphonies of Wind Instruments
Garches, 1920
(rev. 1947)
Duration: 12 min
Original 1920 instrumentation:
3 flutes (3rd doubling piccolo), alto flute, 2 oboes, cor anglais, 2 clarinets in B flat, alto clarinet in F, 3 bassoons (3rd doubling contra bassoon), 4 horns, 2 trumpets in C, trumpet in A, 3 trombones, tuba.
Revised 1947 instrumentation:
3 flutes, 2 oboes, cor anglais, 3 clarinets in B flat, 3 bassoons (3rd doubling contra bassoon), 4 horns, 3 trumpets in B flat, 3 trombones, tuba.
First performance: 10 June 1921. Queen's Hall, London. Conducted by Serge Koussevitzky.
'To the memory of Claude Debussy'

Piano reduction by Arthur Lourié
1920 version:
Full score and parts for hire (except USA).

1947 revised version:
Full score. Pocket score.
Full score and parts for hire.
Edition Russe de Musique
Boosey & Hawkes

A piano reduction of the concluding section of the *Symphonies of Wind Instruments* was published as 'Fragment des Symphonies pour instruments à vent à la mémoire de Claude Achille Debussy' in a supplement to *La Revue musicale,* December 1920, entitled 'Tombeau de Claude Debussy.'

Les Cinq doigts
EIGHT VERY EASY PIECES ON FIVE NOTES
FOR PIANO
Garches, 1921
Duration: 6 min
1. Andantino 2. Allegro 3. Allegretto 4. Larghetto 5. Moderato 6. Lento 7. Vivo
8. Pesante
J. & W. Chester

Transcription
Eight Instrumental Miniatures. See below (1962).

Variation de la fée de lilas from The Sleeping Beauty (Peter Tchaikovsky)
ARRANGED FOR ORCHESTRA BY STRAVINSKY
1921
1.2.1.1. — 4.2.3.1. — Str.

Entr'acte from The Sleeping Beauty (Peter Tchaikovsky)
ARRANGED FOR SOLO VIOLIN AND ORCHESTRA BY STRAVINSKY
1921
2.3.2.2. — 4.2.3.1. — Str.
The orchestrations were made at Diaghilev's request for the Russian Ballet performances
of *The Sleeping Beauty* given at the Alhambra Theatre, London, during November 1921.
Full scores and parts for hire.
Boosey & Hawkes

Suite No. 2
FOR CHAMBER ORCHESTRA
1921
Duration: 5 min
2.1.2.2. — 1.2.1.1. — Perc. Piano — Str.
1. March 2. Waltz 3. Polka 4. Galop
The first three movements are transcriptions of the *Three Easy Pieces* for piano duet. The
fourth movement is a transcription of the Galop from the *Five Easy Pieces* for piano duet.
See above (1914–15 and 1917). *Suite No. 1* was orchestrated in 1925 (see below).
Study score.
Full score and parts for hire.
J. & W. Chester

Mavra
OPERA BUFFA IN ONE ACT
FOR SOPRANO, MEZZO–SOPRANO, CONTRALTO, AND TENOR SOLOISTS AND ORCHESTRA
Biarritz, 1922
(rev. 1947)
Duration: 30 min

(Mavra, Cont'd)

Russian verse libretto by Boris Kochno, based on Alexander Pushkin's *The Little House in Kolomna*.

English translation by Robert Craft

French translation by Jacques Larmanjat

German translation by A. Elukhen

3.3.3.2. — 4.4.3.1. — Timp. — Strings: a solo trio of 2 violins and viola, and a full complement of violoncellos and double basses.

First performance: 3 June 1922. Russian Ballet, Théâtre de l'Opéra, Paris. Conductor: Gregor Fitelberg. Décor and costumes: Léopold Survage.

'À la mémoire de Pouchkine, Glinka et Tschaikovsky'

Vocal score. Pocket score.

Full score and parts for hire.

Edition Russe de Musique

Boosey & Hawkes

Transcriptions

(i) Parasha's Aria

FOR SOPRANO AND SMALL ORCHESTRA

1922–23

Duration: 3 min

Russian, English, French, and German texts

0.2.2.2. — 4.0.0.1. — Strings: a solo trio of 2 violins and viola, and a full complement of violoncellos and double basses.

Full score and parts for hire.

(ii) Parasha's Aria

FOR VOICE AND PIANO

1921–22

Russian and English texts

(iii) Russian Maiden's Song (Parasha's Aria)

FOR VIOLIN AND PIANO

In collaboration with Samuel Dushkin

1937

(iv) Russian Maiden's Song

FOR VIOLONCELLO AND PIANO

In collaboration with Dmitri Markevitch

Edition Russe de Musique

Boosey & Hawkes

Les Noces

RUSSIAN DANCE SCENES WITH SONG AND MUSIC

For soprano, mezzo–soprano, tenor, and bass soli, chorus, four pianos, timpani, and percussion (six players).

Monaco, 1923

Duration: 24 min

(Les Noces, Cont'd)

Russian words adapted by the composer from Russian popular texts collected by Afanasiev and Kireievsky.

French translation by C. F. Ramuz

English translation by D. Millar Craig

German translation by K. Gutheim and H. Krüger

First performance: 13 June 1923. Russian Ballet, Théâtre de la Gaieté Lyrique, Paris. Conductor: Ernest Ansermet. Choreography: Bronislava Nijinska. Décor and costumes: Natalia Goncharova. The pianists were Georges Auric, Edouard Flament, Hélène Léon, and Marcelle Meyer.

'À Serge de Diaghilev'

Vocal score. Full score. Study score. English libretto.

Full score, choral score, and parts for hire.

J. & W. Chester

Note: The sketches for *Les Noces* date from 1914 onward. The vocal score is dated Morges, 1917. At least two different orchestrations were made before the 1923 version.

1917 orchestration for all 4 Tableaux:

3.3.3.2. — 4.4.3.1. + 2 Flügelhorns — Timp. Perc. (1), 2 Harps, Harmonium, Cimbalom, Harpsichord, Piano — Str. (3 violins, 2 violas, 2 violoncellos, 1 double bass).

Choir and soloists as in the 1923 version.

First performance: 11 February 1973. Waldman Auditorium, Columbia University, New York City. Conducted by Robert Craft.

1919 orchestration for the first 2 Tableaux:

2 cimbalom, harmonium, timp., perc. (2), pianola (ossia 2 pianos).

Choir and soloists as in the 1923 version.

J. & W. Chester

Octet

FOR WIND INSTRUMENTS

Paris, 1923

(rev. 1952)

Duration: 16 min

Flute, clarinet in A doubling in B flat, 2 bassoons, trumpet in C, trumpet in A, trombone, bass trombone.

1. Sinfonia 2. Tema con variazioni 3. Finale

First performance: 18 October 1923. Concerts Koussevitsky, Théâtre de l'Opéra, Paris. Conducted by the composer.

Dedicated to Vera de Bosset

Piano reduction by Arthur Lourié. Pocket score.

Full score and parts for hire.

Edition Russe de Musique

Boosey & Hawkes

Concerto

FOR PIANO AND WIND INSTRUMENTS

Biarritz, 1924

(rev. 1950)

Duration: 20 min

3.3.2.2. — 4.4.3.1. — Timp. — Double basses

1. Largo–Allegro 2. Largo 3. Allegro

First performance: 22 May 1924. Concerts Koussevitzky, Théâtre de l'Opéra, Paris. Conducted by Serge Koussevitzky with the composer as soloist.

'À Madame Nathalie Koussevitzky'

Reduction for two pianos. Full score. Pocket score. Full score and parts for hire.

Edition Russe de Musique

Boosey & Hawkes

Sonata

FOR PIANO

Nice, 1924

Duration: 10 min

1. ♩ = 112 2. Adagietto 3. ♩ = 112

First performance: July 1925. Donaueschingen.

'Dédiée à Madame la Princesse Edmond de Polignac'

Edition Russe de Musique

Boosey & Hawkes

Serenade in A

FOR PIANO

Nice, 1925

Duration: 12 min

1. Hymne 2. Romanza 3. Rondoletto 4. Cadenza finale

'À ma femme'

Edition Russe de Musique

Boosey & Hawkes

Suite No. 1

FOR SMALL ORCHESTRA

1925

Duration: 7 min

(Suite No. 1, Cont'd)

2.1.2.2. — 1.1.1.1. — Bass drum — Str.

1. Andante 2. Napolitana 3. Española 4. Balalaika

Study score. Full score and parts for hire.

J. & W. Chester

Suite No. 1 is a transcription of the first four movements of the *Five Easy Pieces* for piano duet. See above (1917).

Otche Nash' — Отче нашъ
FOR S.A.T.B. CHORUS A CAPPELLA
1926
Duration: 1½ min
Slavonic text
Edition Russe de Musique
Boosey & Hawkes

Version with Latin text
Pater Noster
1949
Boosey & Hawkes

Œdipus Rex
OPERA–ORATORIO IN TWO ACTS AFTER SOPHOCLES
Mezzo–soprano, 2 tenors, 2 bass–baritones and bass soloists, narrator, male chorus, and orchestra.
Paris, 1927
(rev. 1948)
Duration: 50 min
Libretto by Jean Cocteau
Sung text translated into Latin by Jean Daniélou
English translation of the spoken text by e. e. cummings.
German translation of the spoken text by L. Thurneiser
An alternative English translation of the spoken text by Carl Wildman, published by Oxford University Press.
3.3.3.3. — 4.4.3.1. — Timp. Perc. (2), Harp, Piano — Str.
First performance (unstaged): 30 May 1927. Russian Ballet, Théâtre Sarah-Bernhardt, Paris. Conducted by the composer.
First performance (staged): 25 February 1928. Krolloper, Berlin. Conducted by Otto Klemperer.
Vocal score. Pocket score. Libretti, Latin, German.
Full score, choral score, and parts for hire.
Edition Russe de Musique
Boosey & Hawkes

Apollon Musagète

FOR STRING ORCHESTRA

Ballet in two scenes

Nice, 1928

(rev. 1947)

Duration: 30 min

The composer suggests 34 players:
8 first violins, 8 second violins, 6 violas, 4 first violoncellos, 4 second violoncellos, 4 double basses.

First performance: 27 April 1928. Library of Congress, Washington, D.C. Conductor: Hans Kindler. Choreography: Adolph Bolm. Décor and costumes: Nicholas Remissov.

Piano reduction. Full score. Pocket score.

Full score and parts for hire.

Edition Russe de Musique

Boosey & Hawkes

Quatre études

FOR ORCHESTRA

1914–29

(rev. 1952)

Duration: 12 min

3.3.4.2. — 4.4.4.1. — Timp. Harp. Piano — Str.

1. Danse 2. Excentrique 3. Cantique 4. Madrid

Nos. 1–3 are orchestrations of the *Three Pieces for String Quartet*. No. 4 is an orchestration of the *Étude* for Pianola. See above (1914 and 1917).

First performance: 7 November 1930. Berlin.

Full score. Pocket score.

Full score and parts for hire.

Edition Russe de Musique

Boosey & Hawkes

Le Baiser de la fée — The Fairy's Kiss

BALLET IN FOUR SCENES

Nice, 1928

(rev. 1950)

Duration: 45 min

3.3.3.2. — 4.3.3.1. — Timp. Bass drum, Harp — Str.

First performance: 27 November 1928. Ballets Ida Rubinstein, Théâtre de l'Opéra, Paris. Conducted by the composer. Choreography: Bronislava Nijinska. Décor and costumes: Alexandre Benois.

'Je dédie ce ballet à la mémoire de Pierre Tchaikovsky en apparentant sa Muse à cette fée et c'est en cela qu'il devient une allégorie. Cette muse l'a également marqué de son baiser fatal dont la mystérieuse empreinte se fait ressentir sur toute l'œuvre du grande artiste.'

(Le Baiser de la fée, Cont'd)
Piano reduction. Pocket score.
Full score, piano reduction, and parts for hire.
Edition Russe de Musique
Boosey & Hawkes

Transcription
Ballad
FOR VIOLIN AND PIANO
Transcribed in collaboration with Jeanne Gautier
1947
Edition Russe de Musique
Boosey & Hawkes

Divertimento from The Fairy's Kiss. See below (1934).

Capriccio
FOR PIANO AND ORCHESTRA
Nice, 1929
(rev. 1949)
Duration: 16 min
3.3.3.2. — 4.2.3.1. — Timp. — Strings: a concertino quartet of violin, viola,
violoncello, and double bass, and a ripieno.
1. Presto 2. Andante rapsodica 3. Allegro capriccioso
First performance: 6 December 1929. Paris Symphony Orchestra, Salle Pleyel, Paris.
Conducted by Ernest Ansermet with the composer as soloist.

Reduction for two pianos. Pocket score.
Full score and parts for hire.
Edition Russe de Musique
Boosey & Hawkes

Symphony of Psalms
FOR CHORUS AND ORCHESTRA
(The chorus should contain children's voices, which may be replaced by female voices if a
children's choir is not available)
Nice, 1930
(rev. 1948)
Duration: 23 min
Latin texts selected from the Vulgate
Part I: Psalm 38, vv. 13 and 14
Part II: Psalm 39, vv. 2, 3, and 4
Part III: Psalm 150 (complete)
5.5.0.4. — 4.5.3.1. — Timp. Bass drum, Harp, 2 Pianos — Violoncellos and Double
basses

(Symphony of Psalms, Cont'd)

First performance: 13 December 1930. Société Philharmonique de Bruxelles, Palais des Beaux Arts, Brussels. Conducted by Ernest Ansermet.

First American performance: 19 December 1930. Boston Symphony Orchestra, Boston. Conducted by Serge Koussevitzky.

'Cette symphonie composée à la gloire de DIEU est dédiée au Boston Symphony Orchestra à l'occasion du cinquantenaire de son existence'

Vocal score by Soulima Stravinsky. Full score. Pocket score.

Full score, vocal score, choral score, and parts for hire.

Edition Russe de Musique
Boosey & Hawkes

Concerto in D
FOR VIOLIN AND ORCHESTRA

Voreppe, 1931

Duration: 22 min

3.3.3.3. — 4.3.3.1. — Timp. Bass drum — Strings (8.8.6.4.4.)

1. Toccata 2. Aria I 3. Aria II 4. Capriccio

There is no dedication, but the score contains the following prefatory note:
'Cette œuvre a été créée sous ma direction le 23 octobre 1931 au concert du Rundfunk de Berlin par Samuel Dushkin auquel je garde une reconnaissance profonde et une grande admiration pour la valeur hautement artistique de son jeu'

Piano reduction. Full score. Study score.

Full score and parts for hire.

Schott

Duo concertant
FOR VIOLIN AND PIANO

Voreppe, 1932

Duration: 16 min

1. Cantilène 2. Eclogue I 3. Eclogue II 4. Gigue 5. Dithyrambe

First performance: 28 October 1932. The Funkhaus, Berlin. Samuel Dushkin and the composer.

Edition Russe de Musique
Boosey & Hawkes

Simbol' vyeri — Символъ вѣры
FOR S.A.T.B. CHORUS A CAPPELLA

1932

Duration: 3 min

Slavonic text

Edition Russe de Musique
Boosey & Hawkes

(Simbol' vyeri, Cont'd)
New version with Latin text

Credo
1949
Boosey & Hawkes
New version with Slavonic text
1964
Boosey & Hawkes

Perséphone
MELODRAMA IN THREE PARTS
For female narrator, tenor solo, mixed chorus, children's chorus, and orchestra
Paris, 1934
(rev. 1949)
Duration: 45 min
French text by André Gide
3.3.3.3. — 4.3.3.1. — Timp. Perc. (2), 2 Harps, Piano — Str.
First performance: 30 April 1934. Ballets Ida Rubinstein, Théâtre de l'Opéra, Paris. Conducted by the composer. Choreography: Kurt Joos. Décor and costumes: André Barsacq.
Vocal score by Soulima Stravinsky. Pocket score.
Full score, choral score, and orchestral parts for hire.
Edition Russe de Musique
Boosey & Hawkes

Bogoroditse D'vo — Богородице Дѣво
FOR S.A.T.B. CHORUS A CAPPELLA
1934
Duration: 1 min
Slavonic text
Edition Russe de Musique
Boosey & Hawkes

New version with Latin text

Ave Maria
1949
Boosey & Hawkes

Divertimento
FOR ORCHESTRA
Symphonic suite from the ballet *The Fairy's Kiss* (1928)
1934
(rev. 1949)
Duration: 20 min
3.3.3.2. — 4.3.3.1. — Timp. Perc. Harp — Str.

(Divertimento, Cont'd)

1. Sinfonia   2. Danses suisses   3. Scherzo   4. Pas de deux (a) Adagio (b) Variation (c) Coda

Pocket score.

Full score and parts for hire.

Edition Russe de Musique

Boosey & Hawkes

Transcription

FOR VIOLIN AND PIANO

Transcribed in collaboration with Samuel Dushkin

Duration: 20 min

Edition Russe de Musique

Boosey & Hawkes

Concerto

FOR TWO SOLO PIANOS

Paris, 1935

Duration: 20 min

1. Con moto   2. Notturno: Adagietto   3. Quattro variazioni   4. Preludio e fuga

First performance: 21 November 1935. Salle Gaveau, Paris. Soulima Stravinsky and the composer.

Schott

Jeu de cartes

BALLET IN THREE DEALS

Paris, 1936

Duration: 24 min

2.2.2.2. — 4.2.3.1. — Timp. Bass drum — Strings (12.10.8.6.6.)

First performance: 27 April 1937. American Ballet, Metropolitan Opera House, New York. Conducted by the composer. Choreography: George Balanchine. Décor and costumes: Irene Sharaff.

Piano reduction. Full score. Study score.

Full score and parts for hire.

Schott

Petit Ramusianum Harmonique

THREE QUATRAINS FOR UNACCOMPANIED VOICE(S)

Paris, 1937

French texts by Charles-Albert Cingria

For C. F. Ramuz's sixtieth birthday

Published in the volume *Hommage à C.-F. Ramuz,* V. Porchet & Cie., Lausanne, 1938. A facsimile of the MS was later published in *Feuilles musicales,* Lausanne, March–April 1962.

Concerto in E flat 'Dumbarton Oaks'

FOR CHAMBER ORCHESTRA

Paris, 1938

Duration: 15 min

Flute, clarinet in B flat, bassoon, 2 horns, 3 violins, 3 violas, 2 violoncellos, 2 double basses

1. Tempo giusto   2. Allegretto   3. Con moto

First performance: 8 May 1938. Dumbarton Oaks, Washington, D.C. Conducted by Nadia Boulanger.

Reduction for two pianos. Study score.
Full score and parts for hire.
Schott

Symphony in C

FOR ORCHESTRA

Hollywood, 1940

Duration: 30 min

3.2.2.2. — 4.2.3.1. — Timp. — Str.

1. Moderato alla breve   2. Larghetto concertante   3. Allegretto   4. Largo — Tempo giusto, alla breve

First performance: 7 November 1940. Chicago Symphony Orchestra, Chicago. Conducted by the composer.

'This symphony, composed to the Glory of God, is dedicated to the Chicago Symphony Orchestra on the occasion of the Fiftieth Anniversary of its existence'

Full score. Study score.
Full score and parts for hire.
Schott

Tango

FOR PIANO

Hollywood, 1940

Duration: 3 min

Mercury Music Corp. (for USA)
Schott (for Germany and UK)

Transcription

FOR CHAMBER ORCHESTRA

1953

4 clarinets in A, bass clarinet in B flat, 4 trumpets in B flat, 3 trombones, guitar, 3 violins, viola, violoncello, and double bass.

First performance: 18 October 1953. Evenings on the Roof concerts, Los Angeles. Conducted by Robert Craft.

Study score. Full score and parts for hire.
Mercury Music Corp. (for USA)
Schott (for Germany and UK)

The Star-spangled Banner (John Stafford Smith)
FOR ORCHESTRA AND MIXED CHORUS (AD LIB)
New harmonization and orchestration by Stravinsky
Los Angeles, 1941
3.3.2.2. — 4.3.3.1. — Timp. — Str.
First performance: 14 October 1941. Los Angeles. Conducted by James Sample.
Mercury Music Corp.

Bluebird pas de deux from The Sleeping Beauty (Peter Tchaikovsky)
TRANSCRIBED FOR SMALL ORCHESTRA BY STRAVINSKY
1941
Duration: 6 min
1.1.2.1. — 1.2.2.0. — Timp. Piano — Str. (5.0.4.3.2.)

The transcription was made (from a piano score) for the Ballet Theatre, New York.
Study score.
Full score and parts for hire.
Schott

Danses concertantes
FOR CHAMBER ORCHESTRA
Hollywood, 1942
Duration: 20 min
1.1.1.1. — 2.1.1.0. — Timp. — Str. (6.0.4.3.2.)
1. Marche — Introduction   2. Pas d'action   3. Thème varié   4. Pas de deux   5. Marche — Conclusion
First performance: 8 February 1942. Werner Janssen Orchestra, Los Angeles. Conducted by the composer.

Reduction for two pianos
Study score.
Full score and parts for hire.
Schott

Circus Polka
FOR ORCHESTRA
Composed for a young elephant
1942
Duration: 4 min

First performed, in an arrangement for wind band and percussion by David Raksin, on 9 April 1942. Barnum and Bailey Circus, Madison Square Garden, New York City. Bandmaster: Merle Evans. Directed by George Balanchine. Elephants trained by Walter McLain. Costumes designed by Norman Bel Geddes.

(Circus Polka, Cont'd)
Version for orchestra, by the composer

2.2.2.2. — 4.2.3.1. — Perc. — Str.

First performance: 13 January 1944. Boston Symphony Orchestra, Sanders Theatre, Cambridge, Mass. Conducted by the composer.

Piano reduction. Study score.
Full score and parts for hire.
Schott

Four Norwegian Moods
FOR ORCHESTRA
Hollywood, 1942
Duration: 8 min

2.2.2.2. — 4.2.2.1. — Timp. — Str.

1. Intrada 2. Song 3. Wedding Dance 4. Cortège

First performance: 13 January 1944. Boston Symphony Orchestra, Sanders Theatre, Cambridge, Mass. Conducted by the composer.
Study score.
Full score and parts for hire.
Schott

Ode
ELEGIACAL CHANT IN THREE PARTS
FOR ORCHESTRA
Hollywood, 1943
Duration: 11 min

3.2.2.2. — 4.2.0.0. — Timp. — Str.

1. Eulogy 2. Eclogue 3. Epitaph

First performance: 8 October 1943. Boston Symphony Orchestra. Conducted by Serge Koussevitzky.
'Dedicated to the memory of Natalie Koussevitzky'
Study score.
Full score and parts for hire.
Schott

Babel
CANTATA FOR MALE CHORUS, MALE NARRATOR, AND ORCHESTRA
Hollywood, 1944
Duration: 7 min

English text from the Book of Moses (Genesis), Chapter 11, vv. 1–9
German translation by L. Andersen

3.2.3.3. — 4.3.3.0. — Timp. Harp — Str.

45

(Babel, Cont'd)

First performance: 18 November 1945. Wilshire–Ebell Theater, Los Angeles. Conducted by Werner Janssen.

Vocal score. Study score.

Full score, choral score, and parts for hire.

Schott

Sonata
FOR TWO PIANOS

Hollywood, 1944

Duration: 11 min

1. Moderato   2. Theme with Variations   3. Allegretto

First performance: 2 August 1944. Edgewood College of the Dominican Sisters, Madison, Wisconsin. Nadia Boulanger and Richard Johnston.

Boosey & Hawkes, Inc. (for USA)

Schott (for Germany and UK)

Scherzo à la Russe
FOR JAZZ ENSEMBLE

Hollywood, 1944

Duration: 4 min

Original version for jazz orchestra:
2.1.0.0. + 2 Alto Sax., 2 Tenor Sax., 1 Baritone Sax. — 1.3.3.1. — Timp. Perc. Guitar, Harp, Piano — Str. (4.0.2.1.1.)

First performance: 5 September 1944. Broadcast on the Blue Network Program by Paul Whiteman's Band.

Symphonic version (1945)
FOR ORCHESTRA

3.2.2.2. — 4.3.3.1. — Timp. Perc. (4), Harp, Piano — Str.

First performance: March 1946. San Francisco Symphony Orchestra, San Francisco. Conducted by the composer.

Reduction for two pianos. Study score (orchestral version).

Full scores and parts for hire.

Boosey & Hawkes, Inc. (for USA)

Schott (for Germany and UK)

Scènes de ballet
FOR ORCHESTRA

Hollywood, 1944

Duration: 18 min

2.2.2.1. — 2.3.3.1. — Timp. Piano — Str.

First stage performance (incomplete): 24 November 1944. Billy Rose's revue, The Seven Lively Arts, Forrest Theater, Philadelphia. Conductor: Maurice Abravanel. Choreography: Anton Dolin.

(Scènes de ballet, Cont'd)

First concert performance: Winter, 1945. New York Philharmonic Orchestra, New York. Conducted by the composer.

Piano reduction by Ingolf Dahl. Study score.
Full score and parts for hire.
Boosey & Hawkes, Inc. (for USA)
Schott (for Germany and UK)

Elegy
FOR UNACCOMPANIED VIOLA (OR VIOLIN)
Hollywood, 1944
Duration: 5 min
First performance: 26 January 1945. Coolidge Auditorium of the Library of Congress, Washington, D.C. Germain Prévost, viola.
'Composée à l'intention de Germain Prévost, pour être jouée à la mémoire de ALPHONSE ONNOU fondateur du Quatuor Pro Arte'
Boosey & Hawkes, Inc. (for USA)
Schott (for Germany and UK)

Symphony in Three Movements
FOR ORCHESTRA
Hollywood, 1945
Duration: 24 min
3.2.3.3. — 4.3.3.1. — Timp. Bass drum, Harp, Piano — Str.
1. ♩ = 160   2. Andante — Interlude — L'istesso tempo   3. Con moto
First performance: 24 January 1946. New York Philharmonic Orchestra, New York. Conducted by the composer.
'Dedicated to the New York Philharmonic Symphony Society'
Full score.
Full score and parts for hire.
Schott

Ebony Concerto
FOR SOLO CLARINET IN B FLAT AND JAZZ ENSEMBLE
Hollywood, 1945
Duration: 11 min
2 alto saxophones, 2 tenor saxophones, baritone saxophone, bass clarinet in B flat, horn, 5 trumpets in B flat, 3 trombones, piano, harp, guitar, double bass, and percussion.
1. Allegro moderato   2. Andante   3. Moderato — Con moto

(Ebony Concerto, Cont'd)

First performance: 25 March 1946. Woody Herman's Band, Carnegie Hall, New York. Conducted by Walter Hendl with Woody Herman as soloist.

Dedicated to Woody Herman

Full score and parts for hire.

Pocket score.

Boosey & Hawkes, Inc. (for USA)
Edwin H. Morris and Co., London (for UK)

Concerto in D

FOR STRING ORCHESTRA

Hollywood, 1946
(rev. 1946)

Duration: 12 min

32 players: 8.8.6.6.4.

1. Vivace   2. Arioso: Andantino   3. Rondo: Allegro

First performance: 27 January 1947. Basler Kammerorchester, Basel. Conducted by Paul Sacher.

'Dédié à la Basler Kammerorchester et son chef Paul Sacher'

Full score. Pocket score.
Full score and parts for hire.

Boosey & Hawkes

Hommage à Nadia Boulanger

FOR TWO VOICES

Hollywood, 1947

Duration: 40 sec

French text by Jean de Meung

Boosey & Hawkes (see p. 8)

Orpheus

BALLET IN THREE SCENES

Hollywood, 1947

Duration: 30 min

3.2.2.2. — 4.2.2.0. — Timp. Harp — Str.

First performance: 28 April 1948. Ballet Society, New York. Conducted by the composer. Choreography: George Balanchine. Décor and costumes: Isamu Noguchi.

Piano reduction by Leopold Spinner. Full score. Pocket score.
Full score and parts for hire.

Boosey & Hawkes

Mass

FOR MIXED CHORUS AND DOUBLE WIND QUINTET

1948

Duration: 17 min

Children's chorus: trebles and altos. Male chorus: tenors and basses.
2 oboes, cor anglais, 2 bassoons, 2 trumpets in B flat, 3 trombones.

First performance: 27 October 1948. Teatro alla Scala, Milan. Conducted by Ernest Ansermet.

Vocal score by Leopold Spinner. Full score. Pocket score.
Full score, vocal score, and parts for hire.

Boosey & Hawkes

The Rake's Progress

OPERA IN THREE ACTS

1948–1951

Duration: 150 min

English libretto by W. H. Auden and Chester Kallman
German translation by Fritz Schröder
French translation by André de Badet
Italian translation by Rinaldo Küfferle

2.2.2.2. — 2.2.0.0. — Timp. Cembalo — Str.

First performance: 11 September 1951. XIV International Festival of Contemporary Music of the Venice Biennale, Teatro la Fenice, Venice. Chorus and orchestra of the Teatro alla Scala, Milan. Conducted by the composer. Director: Carl Ebert. Producer: Nicola Benois.

Vocal score by Leopold Spinner. Pocket score. Libretti, English, French, and German.
Full score, vocal score, choral score, and parts for hire.

Boosey & Hawkes

Transcription
Lullaby
FOR DESCANT AND TREBLE RECORDERS
1960

(A transcription of 'Anne's Lullaby' from Act 3)
Boosey & Hawkes

Cantata

FOR SOPRANO, TENOR, FEMALE CHORUS, AND A SMALL INSTRUMENTAL ENSEMBLE

2 flutes, 2 oboes (2nd doubling cor anglais), and violoncello

1952

Duration: 30 min

Texts selected from anonymous 15th and 16th century English lyrics.

(Cantata, Cont'd)

1. A Lyke-wake Dirge (Versus I), Prelude
2. Ricercar I — 'The maidens came . . .'
3. A Lyke-wake Dirge (Versus II), 1st Interlude
4. Ricercar II — 'Tomorrow shall be my dancing day'
5. A Lyke-wake Dirge (Versus III), 2nd Interlude
6. Westron Wynde
7. A Lyke-wake Dirge (Versus IV), Postlude

First performance: 11 November 1952. Los Angeles Chamber Symphony Society, Los Angeles. Conducted by the composer.

'This Cantata is dedicated to the Los Angeles Symphony Society which performed it under my direction and for the first time on November 11th 1952'

Vocal score. Pocket score.

Full score, vocal score, and parts for hire.

Boosey & Hawkes

Concertino for Twelve Instruments

1952

Transcription of Concertino for String Quartet; see above (1920)

Septet

FOR CLARINET IN A, BASSOON, HORN, PIANO, VIOLIN, VIOLA, AND VIOLONCELLO

1953

Duration: 11½ min

1. ♩ = 88   2. Passacaglia   3. Gigue

First performance: 23 January 1954. Dumbarton Oaks, Washington, D.C. Conducted by the composer.

'Dedicated to the Dumbarton Oaks Research Library and Collection'

Reduction for two pianos. Full score. Pocket score.

Full score and parts for hire.

Boosey & Hawkes

Præludium

FOR JAZZ ENSEMBLE

1953

(Begun 1936–37. Revised, and string parts added, 1953)

Duration: 2 min

2 alto saxophones, tenor saxophone, baritone saxophone, 3 trumpets in B flat, 2 trombones, celesta, guitar, timpani, snare drum, 3 solo violins, viola, violoncello, and double bass.

First performance: 18 October 1953. Evenings on the Roof concerts, Los Angeles. Conducted by Robert Craft.

Full score and parts for hire.

Boosey & Hawkes

Three Songs from William Shakespeare

FOR MEZZO–SOPRANO, FLUTE, CLARINET IN A, AND VIOLA

1953

Duration: 6½ min

1. Musick to heare   2. Full fadom five   3. When dasies pied

First performance: 8 March 1954. Evenings on the Roof concerts, Los Angeles. Conducted by Robert Craft.

'Dedicated to EVENINGS ON THE ROOF (Los Angeles)'

Vocal score. Full score. Pocket score. Parts.

Full score, vocal score, and parts for hire.

Boosey & Hawkes

In Memoriam Dylan Thomas

DIRGE — CANONS AND SONG

FOR TENOR, STRING QUARTET, AND FOUR TROMBONES

1954

Duration: 6 min

Text by Dylan Thomas

1. Dirge-Canons (Prelude)
2. Song: 'Do not go gentle . . .'
3. Dirge-Canons (Postlude)

First performance: 20 September 1954. Monday Evening Concerts, Los Angeles. Conducted by Robert Craft.

Vocal score. Pocket score.

Full score, vocal score, and parts for hire.

Boosey & Hawkes

Four Songs

FOR VOICE, FLUTE, HARP, AND GUITAR

1954

Duration: 4½ min

Phonetic Russian text by the composer

English translation of nos. 1, 2, and 3 by Robert Craft

English translation of no. 4 by Rosa Newmarch

1. The Drake   2. A Russian Spiritual   3. Geese and Swans   4. Tilim-bom

Nos. 1 and 2 are transcribed from *Four Russian Songs,* 1918–19.

Nos. 3 and 4 are transcribed from *Trois histoires pour enfants,* 1917. See above.

Study score.

Full score and parts for hire.

J. & W. Chester

Two Poems of Balmont

Transcribed for high voice and chamber orchestra

1954

See above (1911)

Greeting Prelude

FOR ORCHESTRA

1955

Duration: 45 sec

3.2.2.3. — 4.2.3.1. — Timp. Bass drum, Piano — Str.

First performance: 4 April 1955. Boston Symphony Orchestra. Conducted by Charles Munch.

'For the 80th birthday of Pierre Monteux'

Full score and parts for hire.

Boosey & Hawkes

Canticum Sacrum ad honorem Sancti Marci nominis

FOR TENOR AND BARITONE SOLI, CHORUS, AND ORCHESTRA

1955

Duration: 17 min

Latin texts selected from the Vulgate

1.3.0.3. — 0.4.4.0. — Harp, Organ — Violas and double basses

Dedicatio:
    'Urbi Venetiæ, in laude Sancte sui Presedis, Beati Marci Apostoli'

  I. Euntes in mundum
 II. Surge, aquilo
III. Ad Tres Virtutes Hortationes
    Caritas, Spes, Fides
IV. Brevis Motus Cantilenæ
 V. Ille autem profecti

First performance: 13 September 1956. St. Mark's Basilica, Venice. Conducted by the composer.

Vocal score. Full score. Pocket score.

Full score, vocal score, choral score, and parts for hire.

Boosey & Hawkes

Choral-Variationen über das Weihnachtslied 'Vom Himmel hoch da komm' ich her' (Johann Sebastian Bach)

TRANSCRIBED FOR MIXED CHORUS AND ORCHESTRA BY STRAVINSKY

1956

Duration: 15 min

2.3.0.3. — 0.3.3.0. — Harp — Violas and double basses

German text

First performance: 27 May 1956. Ojai, California. Conducted by Robert Craft.

'Robert Craft gewidmet'

Pocket score.

Full score, choral score, and parts for hire.

Boosey & Hawkes

Agon

BALLET FOR TWELVE DANCERS

1957

Duration: 20 min

3.3.3.3. — 4.4.3.0. — Timp. Perc.(1) Mandolin, Harp, Piano — Str.

First concert performance: 17 June 1957. Los Angeles. Conducted by Robert Craft.

First stage performance: 1 December 1957. New York City Ballet, New York. Conductor: Robert Irving. Choreography: George Balanchine.

'Dedicated to Lincoln Kirstein and George Balanchine'

Reduction for two pianos. Pocket score.

Full score, piano reduction, and parts for hire.

Boosey & Hawkes

Threni: id est Lamentationes Jeremiæ Prophetæ

FOR SOPRANO, CONTRALTO, TWO TENORS, BASS AND BASSO PROFONDO SOLI, MIXED CHORUS, AND ORCHESTRA

1958

Duration: 35 min

Latin texts selected from the Vulgate

2.3.3.0. + Sarrusophone — 4.0.3.1. + Contralto bugle (Flügelhorn) in B flat — Timp. Tam-tam, Harp, Celesta, Piano — Str.

Incipit lamentatio Jeremiæ Prophetæ

  I. De Elegia Prima

  II. De Elegia Tertia

     (a) Querimonia (b) Sensus Spei (c) Solacium

  III. De Elegia Quinta. Oratio Jeremiæ Prophetæ

First performance (dedicated to the memory of Alessandro Piovesan): 23 September 1958. Sala della Scuole Grande di San Rocco, Venice. Conducted by the composer.

'Dem Norddeutschen Rundfunk gewidmet'

Vocal score by Erwin Stein. Full score. Pocket score.

Full score, vocal score, choral score, and parts for hire.

Boosey & Hawkes

Movements

FOR PIANO AND ORCHESTRA

1959

Duration: 10 min

2.2.2.1. — 0.2.3.0. — Harp, Celesta — Str. (6.6.4.5.2.)

1.♪= 110 2. ♩= 52 3.♪= 72 4.♪= 80 5.♪= 104

First performance: 10 January 1960. Stravinsky Festival, Town Hall, New York. Conducted by the composer with Margrit Weber as soloist.

'To Margrit Weber'

Reduction for two pianos. Full score. Pocket score.

Full score and parts for hire.

Boosey & Hawkes

Epitaphium für das Grabmal des Prinzen Max Egon zu Fürstenberg

FOR FLUTE, CLARINET IN B FLAT, AND HARP

1959

Duration: 1½ min

First performance: 17 October 1959. Donaueschingen Festival.

Playing score, for sale or hire.

Boosey & Hawkes

Tres sacræ cantiones (Carlo Gesualdo di Venosa)

FOR MIXED CHORUS A CAPPELLA

The Sextus and Bassus parts from *Sacræ Cantiones,* Naples, 1603, completed by Stravinsky for the 400th anniversary of Gesualdo's birth.

1959

1. Da pacem Domine
2. Assumpta est Maria
3. Illumina nos

First performance: 10 January 1960. Stravinsky Festival, Town Hall, New York. Conducted by Robert Craft.

Illumina nos available separately

Boosey & Hawkes (By arrangement with Ugrino-Verlag, Hamburg)

Double Canon

FOR STRING QUARTET

1959

Duration: 1½ min

First performance: 20 December 1959. Stravinsky Festival, Town Hall, New York.

'Raoul Dufy in Memoriam'

Full score and parts on sale.

Boosey & Hawkes

Monumentum pro Gesualdo di Venosa ad CD Annum

THREE MADRIGALS OF GESUALDO RECOMPOSED FOR INSTRUMENTS BY STRAVINSKY

Hollywood, 1960

Duration: 7 min

0.2.0.2. — 4.2.3.0. — Strings without double basses

1. 'Asciugate i begli occhi.' Madrigale XIV, Libro quinto.
2. 'Ma tu, cagion di quella.' Madrigale XVIII, Libro quinto.
3. 'Beltà poi che t'assenti.' Madrigale II, Libro sesto.

First performance: 27 September 1960. Venice Biennale, Orchestra del Teatro la Fenice. Conducted by the composer.

Full score. Pocket score.
Full score and parts for hire.

Boosey & Hawkes

A Sermon, a Narrative and a Prayer

CANTATA FOR ALTO AND TENOR SOLI, SPEAKER, CHORUS, AND ORCHESTRA

Hollywood, 1961

Duration: 16 min

English texts selected from the Authorized Version of the New Testament and from Thomas Dekker.

2.2.2.2. — 4.3.3.1. — 3 Tam-tams, Harp, Piano — Str. (8.7.6.5.4.)

1. A Sermon (from the Epistles of St. Paul)
2. A Narrative. The Stoning of St. Stephen (from the Acts of the Apostles)
3. A Prayer (from Thomas Dekker)
   Composed 'In memoriam the Reverend James McLane (†1960)'

First performance (preceded by a public rehearsal on 22 February 1962): 23 February 1962. Basler Kammerorchester, Basle. Conducted by Paul Sacher.

'To Paul Sacher'

Vocal score. Pocket score.

Full score, vocal score, choral score, and parts for hire.

Boosey & Hawkes

Anthem 'The dove descending breaks the air'

FOR S.A.T.B. CHORUS A CAPPELLA

Hollywood, 1962

Duration: 2 min

English text by T. S. Eliot, from part IV of 'Little Gidding' in Four Quartets.

First performance: 19 February 1962. Monday Evening Concerts, Los Angeles. Conducted by Robert Craft.

'Dedicated to T. S. Eliot'

Originally published as Appendix B to *Expositions and Developments,* Faber and Faber, London, 1962.

Boosey & Hawkes

Eight Instrumental Miniatures

FOR FIFTEEN PLAYERS

1962

Duration: 6 min

2 flutes, 2 oboes, 2 clarinets in B flat (doubling in A), 2 bassoons, horn, 2 violins, 2 violas, 2 violoncellos.

1. Andantino 2. Vivace 3. Lento 4. Allegretto 5. Moderato 6. Tempo di marcia 7. Larghetto 8. Tempo di tango

First performance (of the first four movements): 26 March 1962. Monday Evening Concerts, Los Angeles. Conducted by Robert Craft.

First complete performance: 29 April 1962. CBC Symphony Orchestra, Massey Hall, Toronto. Conducted by the composer.

'To Lawrence Morton'

(Eight Instrumental Miniatures, Cont'd)

Eight Instrumental Miniatures are transcriptions of *Les Cinq doigts* of 1921. The movements are in a different order from that of the original; and two movements, nos. 2 and 6, have been transposed. No. 8, under the title *Pesante,* was transcribed for an ensemble of twelve players in 1961 and performed in December of that year in Mexico City, conducted by Robert Craft. It was subsequently withdrawn by the composer.

Study score.

Full score and parts on sale or for hire.

J. & W. Chester

The Flood

A MUSICAL PLAY FOR TENOR AND TWO BASS SOLI, NARRATOR, CALLER, SPEAKERS, S.A.T. CHORUS, AND ORCHESTRA

1962

Duration: 24 min

The English text, chosen and arranged by Robert Craft, is derived principally from the Book of Genesis and from the York and Chester cycles of miracle plays (set down between 1430 and 1500)

German translation by Ernst Roth

4.3.4.3. — 4.3.3.1. — Timp. Perc. (3), Xylophone-Marimba, Harp, Piano (Celesta) — Str.

First performance: 14 June 1962. Broadcast on the CBS Television Network, USA. Conducted by Robert Craft. Choreography: George Balanchine. Designer: Rouben Ter-Arutunian.

First stage performance: 30 April 1963. Staatsoper, Hamburg. Conducted by Robert Craft. Production: Gunther Rennert. Choreography: Peter van Dyk. Décor and costumes: Téo Otto.

Vocal score. Pocket score.

Full score, vocal score and parts for hire.

Boosey & Hawkes

Abraham and Isaac

A SACRED BALLAD FOR BARITONE AND CHAMBER ORCHESTRA

1963

Duration: 12 min

Hebrew text from Genesis XXII, vv. 1–19, edited by Dr. Meir Gertner.

3.2.2.2. — 1.2.2.1. — Str.

First performance: 23 August 1964. Ephraim Biran with the Israel Festival Orchestra, Binyanei He'Coma, Jerusalem. Conducted by Robert Craft.

'Dedicated to the people of the State of Israel'

Vocal score. Pocket score.

Full score, vocal score, and parts for hire.

Boosey & Hawkes

Canzonetta (Jean Sibelius, Opus 42a)
TRANSCRIBED FOR CLARINET IN A, BASS CLARINET IN A, FOUR HORNS, HARP, AND DOUBLE BASS BY STRAVINSKY

1963

First performance: 30 September 1963. Monday Evening Concerts, Los Angeles. Conducted by Robert Craft.

Breitkopf und Härtel

Elegy for J. F. K.
FOR BARITONE OR MEZZO–SOPRANO SOLO AND THREE CLARINETS

Clarinets 1 and 2 in B flat, Clarinet 3 in E flat alto

Hollywood, 1964

Duration: 1½ min

English text by W. H. Auden

First performance (of the baritone version): 6 April 1964. Monday Evening Concerts, Los Angeles. Conducted by Robert Craft.

First performance (of the mezzo–soprano version): 6 December 1964. Philharmonic Hall, New York. Conducted by the composer.

Full score and parts on sale or for hire.

Boosey & Hawkes

Fanfare for a New Theatre
FOR TWO TRUMPETS IN C

1964

Duration: ½ min

First performance: 19 April 1964. New York State Theater, Lincoln Center. Robert Nagel and Theodore Weiss.

'To Lincoln and George'

Playing score on sale or for hire.

Boosey & Hawkes

Variations
ALDOUS HUXLEY IN MEMORIAM

FOR ORCHESTRA

Hollywood, 1964

Duration: 5 min

3.3.3.2. — 4.3.3.0. — Harp, Piano — Str.(12.0.10.8.6.)

First performance: 17 April 1965. Chicago Symphony Orchestra, Chicago. Conducted by Robert Craft.

Pocket score.
Full score and parts for hire.

Boosey & Hawkes

Introitus

T. S. ELIOT IN MEMORIAM

FOR MALE CHORUS AND CHAMBER ENSEMBLE

Hollywood, 1965

Duration: 4 min

Latin text from the Missa pro Defunctis

Harp, piano, 2 tam-tams (2 players), 2 timpani (2 players), solo viola, solo double bass.

First performance: 17 April 1965. Chicago Symphony Orchestra, Chicago. Conducted by Robert Craft.

Pocket score.

Full score, choral score, and parts for hire.

Boosey & Hawkes

Canon for Concert Introduction or Encore

FOR ORCHESTRA

1965

Duration: 1 min

3.3.3.3. — 4.3.3.1. — 5 Timp. (1 player), Bass drum, Harp, Piano — Str.

First performance: 16 December 1965. CBC, Toronto. Conducted by Robert Craft.

Composed as a memorial to Pierre Monteux.

The theme of the canon is taken from the finale of *L'Oiseau de feu*.

Full score.

Full score and parts for hire.

Boosey & Hawkes

Requiem Canticles

FOR CONTRALTO AND BASS SOLI, S.A.T.B. CHORUS, AND ORCHESTRA

1966

Duration: 15 min

Latin texts selected from the Missa pro Defunctis

4.0.0.2. — 4.2.3.0. — Timp. (2 players), Perc. (Xylophone, Vibraphone and Bells, 2 players), Harp, Celesta, Piano — Str. (6.5.4.3.2.)

I. Prelude	IV. Tuba mirum	VII. Lacrimosa
II. Exaudi	V. Interlude	VIII. Libera me
III. Dies irae	VI. Rex tremendae	IX. Postlude

First performance: 8 October 1966. Princeton University. Conducted by Robert Craft.

'To the memory of Helen Buchanan Seeger'

Vocal score. Pocket score.

Full score, vocal score, choral score, and parts for hire.

Boosey & Hawkes

The Owl and the Pussy-cat
FOR VOICE AND PIANO
1966
Duration: 3 min
English text by Edward Lear
First performance: 31 October 1966. Monday Evening Concerts, Los Angeles. Peggy Bonini, soprano, and Ingolf Dahl.
'To Vera'
Boosey & Hawkes

Two Sacred Songs (Hugo Wolf, from the 'Spanisches Liederbuch')
TRANSCRIBED FOR MEZZO–SOPRANO, THREE CLARINETS IN A, TWO HORNS, TWO VIOLINS, VIOLA, VIOLONCELLO, AND DOUBLE BASS BY STRAVINSKY
1968
Duration: 5 min
German texts by Paul Heyse and Emanuel Geibel
1. Herr, was trägt der Boden hier . . .
2. Wunden trägst du . . .
First performance: 6 September 1968. Los Angeles County Museum of Art. Christina Krooskos, mezzo–soprano. Conducted by Robert Craft.
'To Marilyn Horne'
Full score and parts for hire.
Boosey & Hawkes

Shortly before his death, Stravinsky was working on transcriptions of four Preludes and Fugues from J. S. Bach's *Das wohltemperierte Klavier* for an orchestra of 3 clarinets, 2 bassoons, and strings: the E minor (Book I, No. 10), D minor (Book II, No. 6), B minor (Book I, No. 24) and C sharp minor (Book I, No. 4). They remain unpublished.

Multilingual Index of Titles

This index is intended to provide as complete a guide as possible to titles of Stravinsky works that have achieved wide currency in English, French, German, Italian, and Russian—whether or not a particular translated form has been cited in the main body of the Catalogue. To that end we have included, not only "official" translations, but versions that may be found in other works of reference, or under which certain pieces were recorded (e.g., *Basle* Concerto, *The Star-faced One*). Each "foreign" title is referred to the form under which the work in question appears in the main body of the Catalogue and in the other indexes. Excerpts and transcriptions of portions of works are also found here crossreferenced to their parent compositions.

     Certain titles of a strictly generic nature (e.g., *Symphonie in C/Sinfonie en Ut/Sinfonia in Do maggiore*, etc.) have been omitted as unlikely to cause confusion to users of the Catalogue, English speaking or otherwise. In contrast to the main Catalogue and the other indexes, numerals rather than letters have been used in translations of titles beginning with a number, for simplicity of reference: thus, *Four Studies* but *4 Études*.

Classified Index of Published Works

Main Title Index